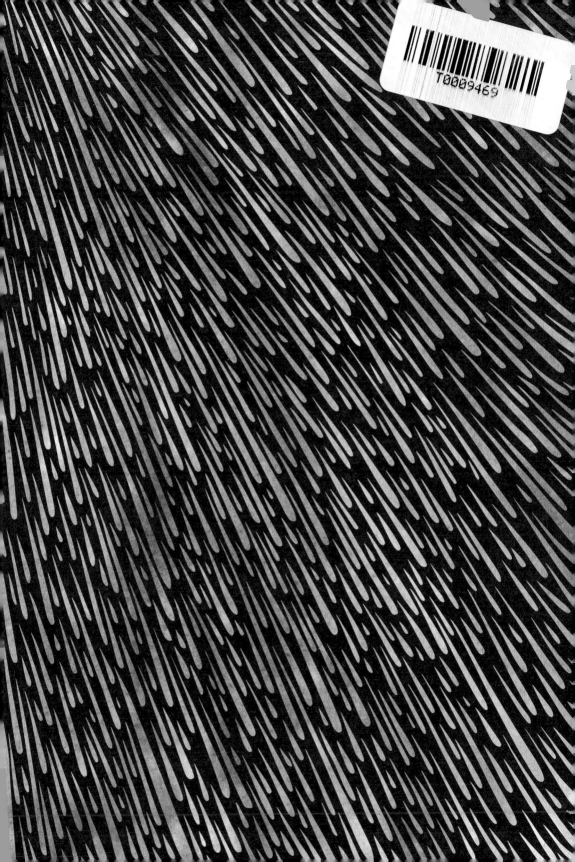

SALISH SEA

1·2·3
SALISH
SEA

A Pacific Northwest
Counting Book

NIKKI McCLURE

little bigfoot
an imprint of sasquatch books
seattle, wa

ONE
Stubby squid
exploring below

2

TWO
Banana slugs
intertwined

3 THREE Lumpsuckers hanging on

4 FOUR
Moon jellies
drifting about

5 FIVE
Salmon swimming home

6 SIX
Nudibranchs
dancing all night

7 SEVEN
Seals
napping all day

EIGHT
8 Kelp crabs lunching in a forest

9

NINE
Orcas
hunting
together

10

TEN
Sand lance
in an auklet's bill

20

TWENTY
Clams for an octopus's feast

50

FIFTY

Surf scoters
diving deep

100

ONE HUNDRED

Sculpins in a
clam garden
pool

500

FIVE HUNDRED

Dunlins flying as one

1,000
ONE THOUSAND

Years of a
cedar tree
sharing life

10,000

TEN THOUSAND
Plankton glowing
at midnight

1,000,000

ONE MILLION

Raindrops returning
to the Salish Sea

Manufactured in China by C&C Offset Printing Co. Ltd. Shenzhen, Guangdong Province, in January 2023

Printed on recycled paper

LITTLE BIGFOOT with colophon is a registered trademark of Penguin Random House LLC

26 25 24 23   9 8 7 6 5 4 3

Editor: Christy Cox
Designer: Anna Goldstein

Library of Congress Cataloging-in-Publication Data
Names: McClure, Nikki, author.
Title: 1, 2, 3 Salish Sea : a pacific northwest counting book / Nikki McClure.
Other titles: One, two, three Salish Sea
Identifiers: LCCN 2020022692 | ISBN 9781632173362 (hardcover)
Subjects: LCSH: Marine animals--Salish Sea (B.C. and Wash.)--Juvenile
   literature. | Sea monsters--Salish Sea (B.C. and Wash.)--Juvenile
   literature. | Counting--Juvenile literature. | Salish Sea (B.C. and
   Wash.)--Juvenile literature.
Classification: LCC QL122.2 .M3764 2021 | DDC 591.77--dc23
LC record available at https://lccn.loc.gov/2020022692

ISBN: 978-1-63217-336-2

Sasquatch Books
1325 Fourth Avenue, Suite 1025
Seattle, WA 98101

SasquatchBooks.com

AUTHOR'S NOTE

The Salish Sea is one of the largest inland seas in the world. It spans from Olympia, Washington, in the south to Campbell River, British Columbia, in the north and west to Neah Bay, Washington. The sea is named in honor of the Coast Salish peoples, who have cared for the water and land since time immemorial.

I live on the shores of this sea in Olympia, home of the Nisqually and Squaxin peoples. My family sometimes sails north up the Salish Sea. There I swim in cold waters with a snorkel and mask and enter a world of kelp forests and clam gardens, ancient walls of stone built to grow clams that still teem with life. Underwater, my community expands and I am just one part of millions.

This is a book of some of my favorite creatures that I share with the Salish Sea. What creatures share the world that you live in? Look around you. Notice. Become aware of your full community. It is bigger than you, or anything human-built.

———————————————————

Illustrations are cut from black paper and colored with watercolor.

Thank you to Jay T. and Finn; Scott Ogilvie; Steven Malk; Beam Paints; Dr. Thomas Mumford; Agathe; and Christy Cox and Anna Goldstein at Sasquatch Books.

———————————————————

Dedicated to Dr. Steven G. Herman who taught me how to count birds.